Grit, Grace, and Gold

Grit, Grace, and Gold

Haiku
Celebrating the Sports of Summer

Kit Pancoast Nagamura

Kodansha USA

Published by Kodansha USA Publishing, LLC
451 Park Avenue South, New York, NY 10016

Distributed in the United Kingdom and continental Europe
by Kodansha Europe Ltd.

Haiku by the following contributors are included by permission of each contributor:
Barnabas I. Adeleke, Elaine Andre, Terry Ann Carter, Kanchan Chatterjee,
Marion Clarke, Terri Hale French, Abigail Friedman, Goran Gatalica,
Nikolay Grank, Lee Gurga, Kotaro Iizawa, Masako Kakutani, Kris (moon) Kondo,
Leonardo Lazarri, Greg Longenecker, Carole MacRury, Marie Mariya, David McCullough,
Marietta McGregor, David McMurray, Yoshie Miyaji, Emiko Miyashita,
Megumi Moriyama, Michio Nakahara, Kazuko Nishimura, Kazuo Oda, Junko Ochi,
Natalia Rudychev, Robin Anna Smith, Alan Summers, Nanae Tamura, Akira Usami.

Lee Gurga's haiku has appeared in *Baseball Haiku*,
edited by Cor van den Heuvel and Nanae Tamura, W. W. Norton & Company,
copyright © 2007 by Lee Gurga, reprinted by permission of the author.

First U.S. edition 2020 by Kodansha USA,
an imprint of Kodansha USA Publishing, LLC

kodanshausa.com

23 22 21 20   5 4 3 2 1

Dedication

When I was six years old
and learning to read, my grandfather told me
I should "start with a book that is worth reading" and
he gave me a small compilation of haiku
in English. This, then, is dedicated to the lasting
influence of books, and to the memory of
Leonard Muller, my beloved Tatie.

六歳の私が読解を学んでいたころ、
祖父は「読むに値する本から始めるといいよ」
と言い小さな英語の俳句集を渡してくれました。
本句集は私の生涯に影響を与えたこの小さな本と、
親愛なる祖父レオナルド・ミュラーの
思い出にささげる。

Contents

Foreword

湾曲し火傷し爆心地のマラソン
　　　　　　　　——金子兜太

twisted and seared
marathon
at ground zero

——Kaneko Tota

translation by Marie Mariya

This haiku compilation which focuses on summer sports has been created by Dr. Kit Nagamura, one of my dearest friends. She is an exceptionally gifted haiku poet, a writer and photographer, and a fascinating person with a good sense of humor.

My initial reaction when hearing about her book of haiku on the theme of sports was one of absolute astonishment. But, her enthusiasm and thoughtfulness made me realize that this is a stunning project.

Haiku poets will know that a *saijiki*, or a compendium of seasonal words (*kigo*) also includes a few sports in each of the four seasons. For example, in spring, "boat race" is a *kigo*. In summer, there are many sports-related *kigo*: swimming, sea bathing, yachting, scull (canoe), rowing, mountain climbing, surfing, diving, water polo, and horse racing. In autumn, we have: sports day, and National Athletic Meet, and in winter, there is rugby, skiing, skating, snowboarding, ice hockey, winter training, mid-winter swimming, and winter sumo training.

It is obvious that the majority of sports *kigo* are for summer and winter, and more than a few poets have composed haiku here and there that were inspired by sports. However, a compilation such as this, focused on summer sports, is unique.

> skinny frog
> hang in there
> Issa is here
>> —Kobayashi Issa
>> translation by Marie Mariya

One of Issa's most well-known masterpieces centers on two male frogs competing. One might imagine that the two frogs are playing sumo or are engaged in a wrestling match. As a humanitarian, Issa of course sided with, and expressed sympathy for, the weaker frog.

> old pond
> a frog jumps in
> —sound of the water
>> —Matsuo Basho
>> translated by Marie Mariya

Basho's masterpiece above has become synonymous with the word "Haiku" itself. The obvious scene is one of a frog leaping into a pond, and yet we can read between the lines a deeper meaning that pertains to our lives and to the truth of the universe. A frog splashes into the water's surface and vanishes under water, and the lingering sound made by the frog remains in our heart. It is a profound philosophical reverberation. One may, of course, read this haiku as one about diving, because actually frogs do dive when they leap into water. And the frog is, in many respects, a metaphor for us, for human beings. Is this then so far away from what we wish to leave behind—a sound of water—when we engage in sports?

The nature of sports is competition. But competition mediated by sportsmanship and ruled by a sense of fair play concludes with a pleasant feeling. We applaud not only the winners, but also we want to give the losers a big round of applause. Athletes offering up their best efforts are beautiful. In addition, "sweat" is a haiku seasonal *kigo* for summer. Haiku poets bracingly enjoy the beauty of an athlete's sweat.

The haiku of Kaneko Tota (see page ix)—twisted and seared / marathon / at ground zero—may pose a query about the true meaning of sports. The marathon at the center of the atomic explosion symbolizes the wish for world peace. The marathon athletes who are running around the war-ravaged town in Tota's poem are certainly a symbol of our hopes for peace. They lead us in thoughts down the road of ancient marathons such as those in Greece.

Sports are fair battles, where the battle is not about ultimate winners and losers, but about vividly beautiful dynamism. This haiku book collects works by Nagamura, a great haiku poet. It also includes the work of 30 poets from Japan and around the world that she has invited to contribute. Her eye, that of a poet and photographer, has celebrated athletic events with splendid examples of "the haiku moment." This book will surely give you a new view of the haiku world—dynamic, youthful, and full of power.

Marie Mariya

まえがき

湾曲し火傷し爆心地のマラソン
　　　　　　　　　　──金子兜太

　この句集は、私の大切な句友のひとり、Dr. キット長村さんが、夏のスポーツを題材とした句ばかりを集めたものです。キットさんは、才能に溢れた俳人であり、ライターでありフォトグラファーです。ユーモアに溢れた魅力的な人。その彼女がスポーツに特化した句集を出したい、と初めて聞いた時は、正直驚きました。でも彼女の熱意とその思いに、私も素晴らしい企画だと思うようになったのでした。その思いの結晶がこの句集です。

　日本には『歳時記』という季節の言葉を集めた書物がありますが、その中にも春夏秋冬、様々なスポーツの季語があります。例えば以下の通りです。

春：ボートレース
夏：水泳、海水浴、ヨット、スカル（カヌー）、ボート、
　　登山、サーフィン、ダイビング、水球、ダービー
秋：運動会、国民体育大会
冬：ラグビー、スキー、スケート、スノーボード、アイ
　　スホッケー、寒稽古、寒中水泳、寒取相撲

圧倒的に夏と冬の季語の多いのが見て取れます。

ですから、スポーツは今までにもたくさん句に詠まれて
きたのですが、夏のスポーツに特化した句集は、今まであ
りそうでなかったユニークなものなのです。

やせ蛙
負けるな一茶
これにあり
　　　　　——小林一茶

　これは小林一茶の代表句ともいえる一句。雄の蛙二匹が
闘っているのを詠んだものです。
　この二匹は相撲、またはレスリングをしているとも読め
ます。ヒューマニストの一茶に相応しく、弱そうなやせ蛙
に寄り添った句。やせ蛙に心情を託しています。

古池や
蛙飛び込む
水の音
　　　　　——松尾芭蕉

　言うまでもありませんが、芭蕉の代表句であり、俳句そ
のものの代名詞とも言える句です。この句はもちろん、蛙
が池に飛び込む情景を詠んだものですが、そこに私たちは
人生の深い意味、宇宙の真理まで読み取れます。一匹の蛙
が水面を切り裂いて水中に消える。蛙が残した水音の余韻
が私たちの心に残る。それは深遠な哲学的な音なのです。
　これは実は、ダイビングの句とも読めると思います。蛙
はダイビングしたのです。蛙は我々人間でもあります。ス
ポーツする人間にも繋がるのではないでしょうか。
　スポーツは闘いです。でもスポーツマンシップに則った

闘いの後は、すがすがしい心持ちが残ります。勝者だけで
はなく、私たちは敗者にも拍手を送ります。懸命に闘う姿
は美しいものです。「汗」は夏の季語。アスリートの汗を
私たちはすがすがしく愛でるのです。

　冒頭に揚げた「湾曲し火傷し爆心地のマラソン」という
金子兜太の俳句はまた、近代スポーツの真の意味を問うて
いるといえないでしょうか。爆心地のマラソンは、平和へ
の願いを象徴するものです。戦争、原爆の被害を受けた町
を走るランナー、それはまさに平和への希望のシンボルで
す。古代ギリシャのマラトンにも通じる姿でしょう。

　スポーツとはフェアな戦いです。その戦う姿は勝者も敗
者もなく平等であり、躍動感に満ち、生き生きと美しいも
のです。

　本句集は、才能溢れる長村の句集です。それと共に世界
中のゲスト俳人の30人もそれぞれの句を寄せています。
俳人でありフォトグラファーでもあるキットさんの瞬間を
捉える確かな目が、句に現れています。様々な競技の華麗
なハイク・モーメントの数々。若さと迫力に満ち、躍動す
る俳句の世界をきっと楽しんで頂けると信じています。

毬矢まりえ

Introduction

I think it's best to start this book with a few quick points. First, I will briefly touch on my approach to the poetic form of haiku in English. No doubt there will be some hullabaloo over the fact that I do not follow the 5-7-5 syllable count that is still taught in schools as the form's main distinguishing feature, and I'll get right into my reasoning on that. Second, I will posit some thoughts on how it is that haiku has emerged as one of the world's most endearing and widely practiced forms of poetry. And finally, I will explain why I've chosen to write haiku on the topic of sports.

Haiku in Japanese language usually conforms to a 5-7-5 count of what are known as "*morae*," or units of sound which may superficially seem like syllables, but are in fact far more intricate sound distinctions. Let's look at the word "Tokyo" for example. In Japanese, Tokyo has five *morae*—to-u-ki-yo-u—and just by using that city's name, you would come to the Japanese language limit for your first line of haiku. In English, you'd rack up a mere two syllables, and merrily continue on to conjure up three more syllables for your first line. Based purely on a 17-syllable counting method, a poet writing in English could easily slip in enough words for *two* haiku in Japanese.

Elementary school teachers perpetuate the 17-syllable rule, perhaps because it's a handy way of introducing the concept of syllables. However, English haiku which follow that rule often are wordier and more complicated than Japanese haiku. This is not to say that brilliant haiku in English cannot be produced with 17 syllables—some well-respected poetry groups still enjoy and excel at using those perimeters—but after nearly 30 years in Japan, I've come to think that briefer poems, far shorter than 17 syllables, better capture the piercing brevity which is the hallmark of traditional haiku.

Next, many people recognize that there is usually a seasonal element in haiku, but few realize that the words which signal the seasons in haiku—known as *kigo*—are agreed-upon terms compiled over the centuries in large dictionaries called *saijiki*. For many poets in Japan, haiku require a seasonal reference that has been established and recorded in a *saijiki*. There are of course poets in Japan and abroad who choose to omit a seasonal reference, but I prefer to include this traditional element for several reasons. First, I enjoy reading the work of my predecessors, and I think referring to poems from the past, the majority of which include *kigo*, is one of the joys of the art. Second, no matter how we abuse it, nature rules our world, and I appreciate a practice that celebrates and observes this. Third, seasonal observations offer a splendid shorthand that transverses boundaries and centuries. No matter where you live, words such as, say, "summer nap," carry a whole load of connotations: warmth, shade, peacefulness, the scent of grass, or perhaps even a sense of safety. By utilizing borderless and timeless references that reverberate effectively, haiku from centuries ago still carry weight today, and the appeal can extend to an international audience.

In the three years that I enjoyed co-hosting NHK World's *Haiku Masters*, an award-winning worldwide broadcast, I learned a great deal about the international attraction that haiku holds for poets. Our show was showered with thousands of poems submitted from every curve of the planet. These held great meaning, in part thanks to the individual talents and sharp observations of the poets, but also due to their focus on seasonal elements, from which we, and our TV viewers, could all draw deep meaning.

Whether you write haiku in three lines, two lines, or a single line (as they usually appear in Japan), whether you employ *kigo* or not, and whether you count the syllables or *morae* of your haiku are all extremely important choices each poet must make, but it is not my aim to police. I've read memorable and remarkable poems that break every rule, to be honest, and I think each poet must discover his or her or their own comfort zone. And, actually, penning an entire book of haiku focused on sports is, judging from the initial reactions of my fellow haiku poets, verging on the radical.

Poetry and Sports might seem like diametrically opposed fields of human endeavor, and yet they have always seemed to me to have essential crossovers. Writing good haiku involves the same attention to grace, balance, strength, bravery, restraint and observation that propels athletes to their peak. The training for both forms of expression is long, and the performance of both is, relatively speaking, brief. Done well, though, the results of both haiku and competitive sports lift our hearts and suffuse us with an appreciation for the complexity, challenges, and beauty of existence.

The appearance of sports in haiku is not entirely without precedence. Masaoka Shiki (1867–1902), the poet responsible for giving haiku its name and long considered one of the four greats (including Matsuo Basho, Yosa Buson, and Kobayashi Issa), wrote haiku on baseball. Cor van den Heuvel and Nanae Tamura co-edited an anthology, *Baseball Haiku*, that collected more than 200 poems on that sport, and even Formula 1 racecar driver Kimi Räikkönen had his thoughts and utterances arranged in haiku-like format to the delight of his fans. What this book does, with gratitude to those who have come before, is expand the arena of subject matter.

In *Grit, Grace, and Gold*, I've invited a fabulous group of award-winning international haiku poets from around the globe to join me in exploring the flexibility of haiku when combined with the inspiration of sports. My hope is that sports players will feel honored, and thanked, for their efforts and awesome inspiration.

はじめに

　まず最初に本書の特徴をお話しすることから始めましょう。英語による俳句の詩形に関する私の取り組み方について簡単に触れます。私が俳句の重要な特徴であり今でも多くの学校で教えられている五・七・五（17音）による韻律を守っていないことに異論があることは想像に難くありませんので、まずはその理由についてお話しします。次に世界中で人々の心を打ち、広く受け入れられている詩形である俳句の広がりについて説明します。そして最後に俳句の題材にスポーツを選んだ理由について述べます。

　日本語の俳句はモーラ（拍）と言われる五・七・五の韻律で作られています。モーラは仮名文字一字に相当する単位のことですが、その数え方はとても複雑なものです。例えば"東京"という言葉を見てみましょう。日本語では東京は単なる都市の名前ですが　ト　ウ　キ　ョ　ウ　と5拍になり、これだけで俳句の上五をとられてしまいます。これが英語では単に二音節で、上五だけで更に三音節を使うことができます。五・七・五（17音）という制約だけを見ても、英語なら簡単に日本語の俳句を二句読むことができます。

　小学校ではこの五・七・五の17音による韻律を教えていますが、それは音節の概念を教えるのに都合が良いからなのでしょう。英語の俳句ではしばしば語数が多く日本語の俳句より複雑になります。だからといって17音で作ら

れていない英語の俳句は良くないとは言えないでしょう。17音の韻律の形で楽しみ優れた俳句を詠んでる権威ある俳句の会もありますが、30年近い日本での暮らしを通して、私は17音よりはるかに短い詩形であっても伝統的な俳句と遜色なく深い洞察を簡潔に表現することは可能であると思うようになりました。

　次に、多くの人は俳句には季節の要素が入っていることを知っていますが、その"季語"が『歳時記』と呼ばれる長い年月をかけ編纂された分厚い辞書のような本に掲載されている俳句の季節を示す言葉であることをご存知の方はあまり多くありません。日本の俳人の多くは、俳句には『歳時記』に採用され記載されている季節感を表現する季語が必要だとしています。なかには日本でも海外でもこの季節感を省略していることがありますが、私がこの伝統的な折々の季節感を俳句に詠み込みたいと思うのには理由があります。第一に、先達が残した過去の作品の多くには季語が入っており、それらは素晴らしい芸術的な喜びを与えてくれるからです。第二に、どんなに私たちが自然を破壊したとしても、この世界は自然の摂理に基づいており、自然を讃えるこの俳句の約束事には価値があると思うからです。第三に、句作において季節を観察することは、境界や時代を超える素晴らしい道筋を示してくれるからです。例えば"夏の午睡"という響きは、住んでいる地域にかかわらず、温もり、日陰、穏やかな静けさ、草の匂い、それからほっとする気持ちなど多くの感覚を内包して運んでくれます。境界や時代を超えた言葉は、はるか昔の感覚を実に効果的に響かせ今に引き寄せることができ、俳句は国を超えて世界の読者の心を魅了するのです。

　三年にわたり、私は、全世界で放送され受賞歴もあるNHKワールドTV『Haiku Masters』での共同司会を務め

させて頂きましたが、この番組を通して、俳句がいかに世界の詩人にとって魅力的な詩形であるかということに気づきました。この番組には地球上の様々な地域からとても多くの詩・俳句の投稿が届きました。詩人個々人の才能や鋭い視点が素晴らしかったということもありますが、詩に込められた細やかな季節感から、その詩・俳句の持つ深い意味を理解することができると分かったことが、私たち番組スタッフや視聴者にとって大変意義深いことでした。

　俳句を三行、二行、一行など何行で書くかということや（日本では通常一行書ですが）、季語やリズムをどう扱うかということは、句作の上で非常に重要な選択要素ではありますが、私は何を取捨選択するべきかについてを決められる立場にはなく、また決めることが本書の目的ではありません。これまでにも、あらゆる制約を破ってはいても、記憶に残る素敵な詩・俳句に触れる機会が数多くありました。正直なところ、詩人たちがそれぞれのコンフォートゾーンを見出すことが大切だと思っています。実際のところ、本書のようにスポーツのみに焦点をあてた俳句の本は、私の親しい俳人たちの最初の反応からみても、一風変わった斬新なものといえるかもしれません。

　俳句とスポーツは人間の行為としては全く逆の分野のようですが、私にはいつでも両者は基本的なところで表現が交差しているように思えるのです。良い俳句を作るには、アスリートが彼らのピークにあるときと同様に、優雅さ、バランス、強靭さ、勇気、自制心、そして観察眼が必要です。両者には長い準備期間を要しますが、パフォーマンス自体は比較的あっという間です。しかし、俳句でもスポーツでも、最高のパフォーマンスは私たちを高揚させ、私たちはその複雑な表現や挑戦するたたずまいの美しさに心を動かされます。

スポーツを詠んだ俳句に関しては先達の作品にも触れておく必要があります。俳句の名づけ親である正岡子規（1867〜1902）は、松尾芭蕉、与謝蕪村、小林一茶とともに四大俳人と称されておりますが、野球を俳句に詠んでいます。コア・バン・デン・フーヴェル（Cor van den Heuvel）と田村七重が共編した俳句集『Baseball Haiku』（ベースボール俳句）には200を超える野球を題材にした俳句が集められていますし、F1レーサーのキミ・ライコネン（Kimi Räikkönen）の考えや発言を俳句風に編集した俳句集があり彼のファンを楽しませています。本書では、このような先達への感謝の意を表すとともに、スポーツを題材とした俳句の領域を広げることに取り組みました。

　『Grit, Grace, and Gold』は、世界各国の受賞歴のある俳人の方々と共に、スポーツから受ける様々な感動を内包する俳句の表現の多様性を探究してきました。俳人たちに素晴らしいインスピレーションを与えてくれるスポーツ競技者の方々にも称賛と感謝の気持ちが伝わることを願ってやみません。

Aquatics

水中競技

navigating
a chlorine sky
by butterfly

掻き分ける
塩素ブルーの空
バタフライで

a stroke of genius—
wet as a brush
the swimmer's hair

天才のストローク
スイマーの髪濡れ
絵筆のよう

medalist
his stroke the butterfly
he has never seen

メダリストのストローク
彼も見たことのない
蝶のごとし

starting block
her toes curl around
the silence

スタート台
彼女の爪先は巻きつく
静けさに

somewhere the smell
of an ex-girlfriend—
water polo caps

どこか
前の彼女の匂い
水球キャップ

—Leonardo Lazzari, Italy

Archery

アーチェリー

still morning
some part of a bird
in the arrow's aim

朝静か
矢の狙うなか
鳥もいて

parting the quiet
of summer air
the shot arrow

夏の気の
静けさ離れ
射る矢

the full-drawn bow
a forest of watchers
below the new moon

引き絞る矢
観客の森は
新月の下

a honeycomb
of golden stingers
archery target

蜂の巣
金の針の
アーチェリーの的

the last arrow
in his right hand—
the lush green fields

右手には
最後の一矢
芝青し

—Megumi Moriyama, Japan

Athletics

陸上競技

splash pattern
sweat streaks the shirt
of the sprinter

スプリンターのシャツに
汗流れ
白絣の模様

false start
the explosive bolt
of early flowers

フライング
分離ボルト
早咲きの花

double rose—
the runner and sighted guide's
winning smiles

二重の薔薇——
ランナーと伴走者
勝利の微笑み

a sprinter's years
consumed in seconds
blackberries

短距離の年月
秒で使い果たす
ブラックベリー

runner's high
snow flurries that know nothing
of the earth

ランナーズ・ハイ風花は地を知らず

—Michio Nakahara, Japan

Badminton

バドミントン

after a drive
one feather floats loose—
molting birdie

　　　　ドライブを掛ける
　　　　羽根一枚ふわり――
　　　　小鳥が落とす

overhead clear
the trajectory of geese
feathers

　　　　頭上のスマッシュをクリア
　　　　雁の軌道
　　　　羽根

damselfly
in her lofty flight
ulterior plans

イトトンボ
高々と飛ぶ
狙い澄まし

summer heat
the last shuttle flies
home faster

シャトルの決定打
矢のごとく
炎え

birdie speed
faster than the bullet train
blossoms in the wake

シャトル
新幹線より速い
つむじ風のなかの花

deepening summer
whiteness of the shuttlecock
struck with a quick leap

夏深む飛び上がり打つ羽根白し

—Nanae Tamura, Japan

Baseball and Softball

野球・ソフトボール

bent blade of grass
the pitcher considering
angles of wind

草の靡く向き
風を読む
ピッチャー

resounding crack
of the ball in the glove—
clouds part

パーン
グローヴに響くボール――
雲割れる

double-header
the smell of leather and grass
in the catcher's mitt

ダブルヘッダー
キャッチャーミットに革と
草の匂い

sliding home—
recklessly seeking safety
headfirst

ホームへスライディング──
セーフを目指しまっしぐら
頭から

pitching change . . .
a butterfly follows a wave
through the upper deck

ピッチャー交代
蝶は乗る
２階席の応援ウェーブに

—Lee Gurga, USA

Basketball

バスケットボール

how sweet
the start of the game—
peach basket*

なんて甘い
ゲームの始まり──
桃のバスケット*

from outside
a few petals blown in
three-pointers

コート外より
花びらの舞い込む
スリーポインター

---

*The origin of basketball started with players
using a peach basket.
バスケットボールは桃のバスケットを使って
始まった。

slam dunker
swinging on the rim
pond ripples

スラムダンカー
リングのリム揺れ
池のさざ波

full-court press
the sneaker squeaks
of starlings

コートに満ちる
スニーカーの軋み
椋鳥

chair-to-chair contact
the clamor of a blocking foul

椅子また椅子鳴らし
ブロッキング・ファウルの抗議

—Robin Anna Smith, USA

Boxing

ボクシング

summer downpour
a practice ring
of heavyweights

夕立ちや
ヘビー級の
練習リング

red and blue
punching one another
purple hydrangeas

赤とブルー
パンチし合う
紫陽花の紫

pop-pop-pop
boxing gloves firing
far-off fireworks

パンパンパン
グローブ火を噴く
遠花火

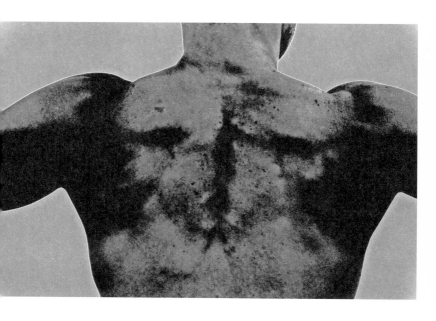

the cutman's cotton
daubing his boxer's face
a sea of clouds

止血用コットン
ボクサーの顔を拭う
雲の海

the boxer knocked out . . .
at the forest's edge
foxgloves

ノックアウト……
森の端っこ
キツネノテブクロ

after the fight the stillness of trees

戦いのあと木々の静けさ

—Abigail Friedman, USA

Canoe and
Kayak

カヌー・カヤック

k-4 canoe sprint
the riverside chase of
ebony jewelwings

四人乗りカヤック
川辺で追いかける
イトトンボ

seeing red
the upstream gate
swinging and swinging

アップゲートの
赤い色
逆巻く逆巻く

kneeling
to the water

to the water
kneeling

屈み込む
水へ

水へ
屈み込む

class V rapids
a kayaker learns to live
in the moment

クラス5の急流
カヤック選手
瞬間を生きる

—Carole MacRury, USA

Cycling

自転車

childhood snapshots
riding backwards
on a bike

幼い日の写真
後ろ向き
車転自

tailwhips*
sudden whirlpools
of verdant air

テールウィップ
不意に渦巻く
若葉風

---

* A tailwhip is a 360-degree rotation of the bike
frame around the front tire, independent of
the rider.
テールウィップとは、空中で自転車だけを360
度回転させる技。

the banked petal
of a wood rose
velodrome

積み重なる花びら
木の薔薇
競輪場

a hawk circles
higher and higher
bike climb

鷹の旋回
高く高く
自転車登りゆく

—Greg Longenecker, USA

Diving and
Artistic Swimming

飛び込み・アーティスティックスイミング

synchronized swimmers
two girls in the stands
point their toes

シンクロの
二人の少女
つま先立つ

controlled fall
tucked against the
heavy air

重い空気を破り
一心に落ちる
身を縮め

disappearing
into a blue flower
splashless entry

消えゆく
青い花のなかへ
飛沫なく

sudden bubbles
from her mouth
in birth waters

口からあふれ出る
きらめくあぶくのかけら
羊水の中

—Masako Kakutani, Japan

Equestrian Events

馬術

winter morning
the white breath
of a breathless horse

冬の朝
息切らす馬
息白し

horse and rider
rush the hedge
faith airborne

馬も騎手も
障害物へと疾走――
信じて飛翔

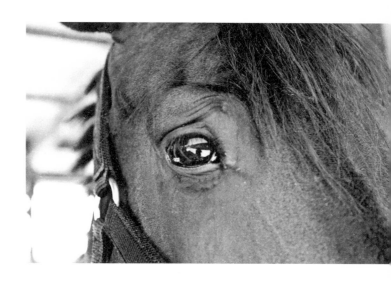

horse and rider
dressed for show . . .
the fly on the wall

人馬とも
正装し……
フェンスには蝿

horse listens
to the slightest touch—
summer breeze

夏の風微かに触るる音馬聞けり

—Marie Mariya, Japan

Fencing

フェンシング

iris leaves
bright blades
en garde

菖蒲の葉
きらめく刃
アン・ギャルド

silver rain
in sheets and sheets
the swift passé

銀の雨
すっすっと
素早いパッセ

the foil*
pinpoints his chest
lightning strike

フルーレ*
彼の胸を一突き
電光石火

thrust in
the afterimage
of fencing

打ち込みし残像冴ゆるフェンシング

—Kazuko Nishimura, Japan

*The foil is the thinnest and lightest of
 swords in fencing competitions.
 フレールとは剣の種類。突き用の細く
 しなるもの。

Football (Soccer)

サッカー

practice hours
in frying heat
la croqueta*

炎暑に
何時間も練習
クロケッタ*

---

*La croqueta, also known as a double-touch,
is an evasive dribbling move.
クロケッタとは、フェイントを使い、ドリ
ブルでかわしていく技術。ダブルタッチ。

feint
the nearly fall
rain

フェイント
秋迫る
雨

holding his shin
the diver* rolls and sucks in
moldering leaves

脛押さえ
うずくまってみせる
枯葉

soccer cheers
on a summer's day
pigtails

夏の日のサッカー声援おさげ髪

—Junko Ochi, Japan

---

*A diver is a player who pretends to fall, for
 the sake of drawing a foul.
 ダイバーとは、ファウルを受けた振りをして
 転倒することを繰り返す選手。

Golf

ゴルフ

the ball's path
through morning dew
the map of a moment

ボールの印す道
朝露をわけ
一瞬の地図描く

several raindrops
earn the distinction:
hole in one

雨粒の数滴が
勝ち取る
ホールインワン

all the sand
of her summer
in the bunker

彼女の夏の砂
バンカーの
砂ばかり

securing footing
he waits for his mind to grow
greener

足元を確かめ待つ
心も
グリーンになるまで

deep tree shade
where a wild swing
goes astray

暗い木陰
夢見る
イーグルの

alchemy:
I turn wood to iron
into an eagle

ウッドをアイアンへ
錬金術──
イーグル狙う

—Alan Summers, U.K.

Gymnastics

体操競技

balance beam
between earth and clouds
lightsome egret

平均台
天と地のあいだ
軽やかな白鷺

the vault
a vast summer sky
traveled by toes

天蓋へ
夏空広し
駆ける爪先

rings
the proposal
of strength

輪と輪
見せつける
筋力

letting go
first note of music
for floor routine

前奏に
耳を澄ませる
床運動へ

—Natalia Rudychev, Russia and USA

Handball

ハンドボール

resin-coated ball
   fumbled fragrance
of forest

         樹脂塗りボール
           とり落とす
         森の匂い

                a backward pass
                the essence of progress
                river eddies

                      バックパス
                     前進のため
                    川は逆巻く

wingman's
horizontal attack
scissortail flycatcher

ウィングの
サイドアタック
シザーテイルヒタキ

a little underhandedness best practice handball

適度なアンダーハンド　ハンドボールに最適

—Marion Clarke, Ireland

Field Hockey

ホッケー

overhead
the sea hawk eyes
the net

オーバーヘッド
鳶の目
ネットに

practice clicks
of a drag flick*
mowing grass

練習の音
ドラッグフリック*の
芝生

---

*The drag flick is a shooting technique
 often used from the penalty area.
 ドラッグフリックとは、ペナルティーエリ
 アのシュートテクニック。

hocquet stick*
sheparding the ball
around the sheep

ホッケーが操る
いにしえは羊
今はボールを

---

*A hocquet stick is like a shepard's hook,
and was the origin of the hockey stick.
ホッケーのスティックは羊飼いの杖に似
ており、その起源となっている。

tick tock
the flick
a golden fly

ティックトック
フリック
金の蝿

light rain
an Indian dribble*
down the pitch

小雨
インディアンドリブル*
ピッチを

—Terri Hale French, USA

---

*Indian dribble is a technique which originated in India.
インディアンドリブルとは、体の左右交互にボールを動かしながら
進むドリブル。またドリブルには滴り（季語）という意味もある。

Martial Arts

武道

a silk moth
struggles to free her wings
judo-gi

蚕
羽根をほどこうともがく
柔道着

the forking dives
of a kingfisher
karate kata

突き刺す
カワセミ一閃
空手の型

ippon
the sound a lotus
opens

イッポン
蓮の花
開く音

bright blue flying from side kicks gladiolas blossom

瑠璃色空中飛び蹴りグラジオラス

the old black belt,
turning white again

古い黒帯
また白に変わる

—David McCullough, Northern Ireland

Multisports

複合競技

hours of sweat
evaporate on the road
in the runners' wake

幾時間もの
ランナーたちの汗
道路からあがる

so much dust raised
Herodotus's story
running round the world

激しい土ぼこり――
ヘロドトス神話
世界駆け巡る

olives shade
those who walk home
the marathon's length

オリーヴの木陰
家路へと
マラソンの距離をゆく

carrying news
the night marathoner
tastes brine

知らせ運ぶ
夜通しのマラソン──
潮の味

here comes
the uphill
sneakers gleaming white

スニーカー白く光りて上り坂

—Marie Mariya, Japan

Rowing

ボート

vernal equinox
trying for balance
either / oar

春分
バランス取ろうと
オールとオール

glassy waves . . .
the backward finish
of a shell

艶めく波……
後ろ向きにフィニッシュ
シェル艇

egret flight
a perfect pause
between strokes

白鷺飛ぶ
見事に止まる
ストロークの合間に

spring sculls*
the shush of moving
clouds

跳ねるスカル*
シュッシュッと動く
雲

---

*Scull is a lightweight competition rowboat.
　スカルとは、ボート競技の種目。

halos
where their oar blades touch
water striders

光の輪
オールの先触れる
あめんぼう

tracing a line
through the river's rose sunset
a team of scullers

水尾をひく
薔薇色の川面の夕日に
スカルチーム

—kris (moon) kondo, USA and Japan

Rugby

ラグビー

scrum
a centipede
on the ball

スクラム
ボールの上の
百足

heat lightning
the zigzagging bolt
trying to ground

熱き稲妻
ジグザグの一団
トライへ

shaking out
a mini-pitch of dirt
from scrum pockets

はたき出す
土を少し
スクラムのポケットから

summer sale
the mall
a maul

サマーセール
モール（ショッピングモール）
モール（ラグビーの密集戦）

lost ball
behind storm clouds
a summer moon

ロストボール
嵐雲の後ろから
夏の月

passing back
to sweep forward
winds in willows

後方パス
驀進のため
柳風

game is over
the deep furrows
on the pitch

ノーサイド
深い爪痕
コートの土に

—Nikolay Grankin, Russia

Sailing

セーリング

spring equinox
a faint luff in the sail
mid-tack*

春分
帆を開く
船首が曲がりだす（タッキング*）

flying fish
the trapeze† crew too
skim salt spray

飛び魚
トラピーズ†クルーも
潮の飛沫をすくう

wing and wing‡
white magnolia petals
spill wind◇

ウィングとウィング‡
白マグノリアの花びら
スピル風◇

---

*Tacking is a technique used to sail in a zigzag course into the wind. As the boat turns
into the wind each time, the sails are momentarily emptied.
タッキングとは船首を風上に向けて旋回させ、ジグザグに進ませるテクニックのこと。
†The trapeze crew, secured by harnesses, hang outside the sailboat to maximize boat balance.
ハーネスで体を支えながらマスト上部のロープを引き、ぎりぎりまで艇外に身を乗り出し
てボートのバランスを取るクルーのこと。
‡Wing and wing is when the mainsail and jib are set on opposite sides of the boat.
ウィングとウィングとは、メインセイルと前帆を船の反対側に設置すること。
◇Spill wind is the wind not caught by sails.
スピル風とは、メインセイルと前帆の間を吹き抜ける風。

when the truth is told—
heavy swells
on a dead run

ほんとを言えば──
重いうねり
風下に横揺れ

dark green winds
your hand practices a capsize
in the bath

青嵐
君はぐいっと手を返す練習
湯船で

shark's teeth
a line of laser boats
await the gun

レーザー級ボートの列
サメの歯
ピストルを待ち受ける

stiff wind
tilting your ear
toward the better course

烈風
耳を水面へ倒す
もっと良いコースへと

feet leave the deck
the boat falls off a wave
at twice hull-speed*

デッキを足が離れ
ボートは波に落ちる
ハルスピード*の二倍で

—Elaine Andre, USA

---

*Hull-speed is the estimated maximum speed for any sailing vessel.
ハルスピードとは、ヨットが水を押しのけて走ることができる最大速度。造波抵抗理論。

Shooting

射擊

double trap
male and female
equal shots

ダブルトラップ
男と女
同点

clear blue sky
from deep within
comes the bullet

透き通る
空の奥から
弾丸発射

rifle thunder
a tiny pond stippled
with pellets

ライフル轟く
池にさざ波立つ
弾丸で

with one shot
she
returns dust to dust

一撃で
彼女は
塵は塵に

shotgun competition
between the trap houses*
overlapping shadows

ショットガン競技
トラップハウス*の間を縫い
重なり合う影

—Goran Gatalica, Croatia

---

*A trap house is the enclosure from which clay
targets are released.
トラップハウスとは放出機を納めた地下施設。

Skateboarding

スケートボード

knuckles graze
the rising sun
half pipe

指のかすめる
ライジングサン（朝日）
ハーフパイプ

hunting the streets
for rails and curbs
summer moon

街中を探す
レールや縁石を求めて
夏の月

hot gusts
litter the bowl* with trash
switch stance

熱風が
ボウル*にごみを撒き散らす
スイッチスタンス（逆向きスタンス）

lip trick†
on the tip of your tongue
what you almost say

リップスライド†
舌先まで出かかる
言おうとしたことが

---

* A bowl is a skate park feature, with dramatically curved walls.
ボウルとは「パーク」で様々な斜面（アール）の入り交じった複合的な窪地のこと。
† A lip trick is any trick done at the edge of a bowl or skate ramp.
リップスライドとは、バックサイドにあるセクションへ身体をバックサイドに90度ひねり、
セクションをまたぎボードスライドさせるテクニック。

climbing the wall
flowering in the breeze
an eggplant*

ウォールを登る
そよ風に花開く
エッグプラント*

down the handrail
a skateboarder's somersault
empty cobweb

ハンドレールへ
スケートボード宙返り
蜘蛛の囲　空に

—Emiko Miyashita, Japan

---

*An eggplant is a trick performed by doing a one-armed
handstand on the coping.
エッグプラントとは、コーピングを片手で掴んで逆立ちする技。

Sport Climbing

スポーツクライミング

all about the leap
toward positivity
passionflower tendril

飛びつくのみ
あれなら掴める
時計草

speed climbing
the slightest difference
between twins

スピードクライミング
僅差
双子のよう

a pause to breathe
at the crux
a bit of Elvis leg

息をつぐ
難所で
プレスリーの足のよう

autumn light
the fierce hold of
an untried route

秋の光
険しいホルダー
まだゆかぬ道

bouldering
a problem solved
with two fingers

ボルダリング
難問を解く
二本の指で

flash*
her climb unflawed beta†
silverfish

　　　　一撃*
　　　　彼女の昇りの完璧なベータ†
　　　　紙魚

unzipped parka
at the world wall climbers meet—
panorama breeze

　　　　パーカーのジッパーを開け
　　　　世界の壁クライマーと出会う
　　　　パノラマのそよ風

　　　　—David McMurray, USA

---

* Flash is when a wall is scaled on a first try without falling.
課題やルートを一回目で完登すること。
† Beta refers to information gleaned, later useful to mastering a climb.
ベータとはボルダリングで情報のこと。

Surfing

サーフィン

forked-tail swifts
the spray of cutbacks*
on the wave's face

アマツバメ
カットバック*の飛沫
波の面に

fins out for air—
from the whiteout foam
only the surfboard

宙に飛ぶ——
水しぶきのホワイトアウトから
サーフボードのみ

---

*A cutback is when a surfer goes down a wave, but turns quickly to return
 up the face of the wave, then curves down again.
 カットバックとは波に乗り戻ってくること。

backdoor* exit
the ocean's aqua roof
hung with chandeliers†

バックドア*から脱出
波の大天蓋
掛かるシャンデリア†

working the small wave
flow
with what comes

小波に
乗る
「受け給う」

---

*A backdoor ride involves pulling into a barrel from behind the section.
バックドアとは、波のピークの後ろ側、奥のこと。
†Chandeliers are light-lit waters falling at the opening of a tube.
シャンデリアとは、筒状の中空の波の出口に降り注ぐ恐るべき水のカー
テンのこと。

duck dive*
knowing just when to go
below it all

ダックダイブ*
ぐっと潜る
時は今

autumn waves
send arrows from the bow
surfers

サーファーに
弓張るやうな
秋の波

—Akira Usami, Japan

---

*A duckdive is a technique to get under waves while paddling out to a
  good surfing zone.
  ダックダイブとは水中に潜り、波を乗り越えていくためのテクニック。

NOTE: Usami wrote this at Yuigahama in Kamakura, where a crescent-
shaped beach popular with surfers was once the area used for the practice
of horseback archery, during the Kamakura Period, 1185–1333.

鎌倉の由比ヶ浜は三日月形でサーファーの間では有名。
また鎌倉時代（1185〜1333 年）には武道、殊に流鏑馬に使われた。

Table Tennis

卓球

teen girls
light talk back and forth
before the smash

ことばを交わす
少女たち
スマッシュ前

penhold
she delivers a new chapter
on spin

ペンホルダー
繰りだす新手の
スピン技

pivot* steps
and ladder drills*
hot peppers in his sweat

　　　　ピボット*ステップ
　　　　ラダートレーニング*
　　　　彼のスウェットに唐辛子

---

* Pivot and ladder drills are footwork training skills, one
featuring twists on a single leg, and the other quick steps
around a ladder-like diagram on the floor.
ピボットとは軸足を中心とした回転。ラダートレーニング
とは梯子を地面に置いての練習。

pinga-ponga-pinga-ponga
pinga   ponga   pinga   ponga   pinga
pan!

ピンガ、ポンガ、ピンガ、ポンガ
ピンガ　ポンガ　ピンガ　ポンガ　ピンガ
パン！

bonus points
after an upset a player
wipes his eyes

ボーナスポイント
苛立つ選手
目を拭う後に

—Marietta McGregor, Australia

Tennis

テニス

dropshot
set down by design
a single green plum

ドロップショット
狙い澄まし
青梅ひとつ

service swing
into the sun
palm frond

打ち込むサービス
太陽へ
椰子の葉

little cuckoo
love love
he sings out

小さきカッコウ
ラブ　ラブ
と歌う

clay court
cicadas emerge
for the match

クレーコート
蝉が現われる
試合に

summer skies
remembering breathlessness
ah, tennis

夏空に
思い出すはずむ息
テニスかな

—Kazuo Oda, Japan

Track and Field

陸上競技

summer dolphins
the fittest jumper's
reverse torque

夏のイルカ
鍛え抜かれたジャンパー
背面回転力

hurricane's eye
the organized axis
of a shot putter

ハリケーンの目
ぶれぬ軸
砲丸投げ選手

her coach's critique
a flea in her ear—
long jumper

コーチの苦言
幅跳選手の耳のなか――
ノミのジャンプ

hurdles
trying to get over
coming in last

超えよう
最下位の
ハードルも

July
the sun's midday ray
a javelin

七月の
真昼の光線
一条の槍

heavy heads vaulting sky high sunflowers

天空に弧を描く重い首　ひまわり

leaving
the front-runner's wind-shadow—
bell lap

去りゆく
先頭走者の風―影―
最終周回

—Barnabas I. Adeleke, Nigeria

Volleyball

バレーボール

bottle rocket sizzles up—
waiting for the bang
but . . . dink*

ロケット花火
待ち構える
と……フェイント

from the spike
a white sand splash
salty winds

スパイク
飛び散る白砂
潮風

---

*A dink is an unexpected light touch return,
just barely over the net.
強打と見せかけて相手コートに軽く落とすこ
と。フェイント。

sitting volleyball
the libero's dig
white summer sun

シッティングバレーボール
リベロのディグ（レシーブ）
夏の白い太陽

sway
of the volleyball net
June breeze

揺れる
バレーボールネット
６月のそよ風

—Terry Ann Carter, Canada

Weightlifting

ウェイトリフティング

hefting
the August mountain
Hercules beetle

持ち上げる
八月の山
ヘラクレスオオカブト

loaded barbells
the subtle curve
of earth

バーベル
ゆるいしなり
地球の

thin branches
featherweight breeze
lifts them

細枝を
持ち上げる
フェザー級のそよ風

summer reunion
the smell of chalk and sweat
in the knurling

夏の再会
チョークと汗の匂いの
ローレットの刻みに

raise the barbell
to the height
of the moon

バーベルを月の高みに差し上ぐる

—Kotaro Iizawa, Japan

Wrestling

レスリング

sultry heat
inside the gym
losing one's grip

館内の
むっとする暑さ
グリップをなくす

5-point takedown
staring at his rival
the stag beetle

五点テークダウン
ライバルを睨む
くわがた虫

par terre*
the dry dirt turned over
in an evening downpour

パーテール*
立ちのぼる砂埃
夕立に

*Par terre is when one wrestler is required to get on all fours in
a defensive position, with opponent in offensive position. It's is
sometimes ordered to stimulate competition.
パーテールとは選手が四つん這いになり、もう一方の選手が反則
で警告を受けたあと、命じられる構えのこと。

the man who pins him
painted on the other side
Greek vase

組み伏せる
男の絵
ギリシャ壺のむこう側

after the handshake
two sweating bodies locked
in arm drags*...

握手のあと
汗まみれのボディロック
アームドラッグ*で……

—Kanchan Chatterjee, India

---

*An arm drag involves pulling one's opponent's arm
 to gain advantage.
 アームドラッグとはレスリングでは手繰りのこと。

Spectating

観戦

late afternoon sun shaft
sneaks toward
a vacant front seat

午後遅くの陽の矢
忍び寄る
前列の空席へ

blue safety mats
reflected in camera lenses
a bed of irises

青のセーフティーマット
カメラレンズに映る
アイリスの花壇

supine he powerlifts* his mother up from her chair

あおのけにパワーリフト*バーベルも応援席の母も

sunglasses
hidden tears for another team's
injured player

敵陣の
ケガ人への涙隠す
サングラス

---

unknown anthem
imagining that country's
summer hills

耳慣れぬ国歌
その国の
夏山に思い馳せ

moon flower
the perfume and soy sauce
of someone nearby

ユウガオ
香水とソイソースの匂い
近くの誰かから

stadium lights off
summer night glimmers
of grace, grit, and gold

スタジアムの光消え
夏の夜瞬く
雅、氣、金
みやび き きん

Acknowledgements

Even the shortest of poems has a long list of influences behind it, and for a collection like this, I have many extremely talented people to thank for their help and selfless gifts of time. I share the creative limelight with my fellow poets around the world, whose short bios follow these acknowledgements and whom I hope you will seek out for fuller knowledge of their works.

The sterling team members at Kodansha USA Publishing have been constant, patient, and super supportive champions throughout the process of creating this book; it is their belief and trust in me that has kept me firmly on track each step of the way. The book's content designer, Toyoko Kon and cover designer Takuma Yamanaka are both so visually talented that I feel fortunate to have their sensitivities on display here.

A bilingual book such as this requires the absolute rarest of translators, ones who know not only two languages inside and out, but also have experience writing haiku themselves. I am beyond grateful to Marie Mariya and Megumi Moriyama, widely published poets both, who have brought their keen insight, delicate touch, and gutsy humor to every page of this work; I simply could not have done this without them. I am also grateful for the keen eye and generous spirit of Masako Kakutani, who read this manuscript with an open heart and mind, and offered her generous comments. Yasushi Sudo patiently urged me to get this ball rolling (only took four years) and Ed Turner gave of his precious time for valuable feedback. I'd like to thank Nobuyuki Ikegami, who reminded me of all that haiku can convey, and Kelly Godbout who years ago prodded me to make a record of the daily haiku I write, and put it in a book. To Tim Bunting, a Yamabushi training in the mountains of Dewa Sanzan, I am indebted for his explanation of the concept of *uketamo*, or accepting whatever comes, with gratitude.

Producer Yukiko Narumi took a chance casting me as a co-host of NHK World's *Haiku Masters*, and revealed to us and viewers around the globe how far-reaching haiku's influence is. My co-hosts Michio Nakahara and Kazuko Nishimura were wonderful masters to work alongside, and I thank them for including me in their lessons. Among those teachers I also tip my hat to are Abigail Friedman, Emiko Miyashita, Elaine Andre, and Gabi Greve.

To bring beauty to each chapter head, I've been lucky to have Master Calligrapher Yoshie Miyaji provide creative and vibrant kanji characters, inked on sheets of paper handmade by the artisans at Ozu Washi.

I've also been able to arrange and shoot photos thanks to assistance from a broad range of people, including Katharine and David Muller, Yoshie Morimura, Captain Satoshi Suzuki, Peggy Kline and her show horse Grady, Chiharu Lorenzoni, Lance Tan, Sergei Golubitsky, Ginny Tapley

Takemori, Takuma Yamanaka, Nobukazu Kawasaki, Betsy Rogers, Susan Griffin, and a special shout out to Jin-san and Sakai-san at Gold's Gym for their time and kindness.

I'm terribly lucky to have a mother, Hélène Pancoast, and mother-in-law, Ichiko Nagamura, who are both strong and influential women, who have urged me on like Amazons. My son Léo has kept me from taking myself too seriously, while nonetheless reminding me that the work I am doing is serious. Last, but never least, is my husband, Mitsuhiro, who gives me space to work, cooks something when I forget to eat, and who actually started this whole project by suggesting I write a book centering on English terms used in sports. This might not be what he had in mind, but if it pleases him, I will be deeply satisfied.

あとがき

　俳句は最も短い詩ですが、とても多くの人々からの刺激や影響によって支えられています。本書の刊行にあたり、才能にあふれた多くの人々が時間を惜しむことなく協力してくださったことに大変感謝しております。世界中の詩人・俳人の仲間たちと創造性に満ちた時間を持つことができました。「あとがき」の後にこの仲間たちの簡単な経歴を掲載しておりますので、彼らの作品についてより一層理解を深めて頂ければ幸いです。

　本書の刊行に際しては、Kodansha USA Publishing の素晴らしいメンバーが、終始誠意をもって辛抱強く私を励ましサポートしてくれました。コンテンツデザイナーの Toyoko Kon 氏と表紙デザイナーの Takuma Yamanaka 氏は、視覚的センスに長けており、両氏の感性をここに披露できたことは大変幸運であったと感じております。

　このような二言語による俳句の本を完成させるためには、日本語と英語の両言語に精通し、かつ自身も実績のある俳人である翻訳者が必要です。翻訳を担当してくださった Marie Mariya 氏と Megumi Moriyama 氏には言葉では言い尽くせないほど感謝しております。お二人ともご自身の俳句集を出版されており、全てのページに深い洞察と繊細さ、そしてツボを押さえたユーモアを交えてくださいました。お二人のご協力がなければ本書を完成することはできませんでした。原稿にお目通しいただき、率直で寛大な

コメントをくださった Masako Kakutani 氏の慧眼と惜しみ
ないご尽力にも心より感謝申し上げます。

　Yasushi Sudo 氏は、この企画が実現できるように粘り
強く促してくださり（最終的には4年かかりましたが）、
また Ed Turner 氏からは、お忙しい中貴重な意見や感想を
いただきました。俳句の持つ伝える力に気付かせてくれた
Nobuyuki Ikegami 氏、そして以前、私に書いたものを記録
するように促してくれた Kelly Godbout 氏にも感謝いたし
ます。何事も感謝の心を持って受け入れるという「うけた
もう」の考え方を教えてくださった出羽三山で山伏として
修業中の Tim Bunting 氏には深い恩義を感じております。

　NHK ワールド TV『Haiku Masters』の共同司会者として
私を抜擢してくださったプロデューサーの Yukiko Narumi
氏は、私たち番組スタッフや世界中の視聴者に、俳句の影
響がどれほど遠くまで及んでいるかを番組を通して発信
してくださいました。一緒に番組の司会を務めた Michiko
Nakahara 氏と Kazuko Nishimura 氏は素晴らしい俳句の達
人で、お二人の俳句のレッスンに加わる機会を得ることが
でき、とてもうれしく思っております。先生方の Abigail
Friedman 氏、Emiko Miyashita 氏、Elaine Andre 氏、Gabi
Greve 氏にも感謝の意を表したいと思います。

　書道家の Yoshie Miyaji 氏は、小津和紙の職人が漉いた
和紙に墨で各スポーツを表す漢字を生き生きと書いてくだ
さり、各章の中扉に美しさを添えてくださいました。

　本書に掲載した写真の撮影は多くの方のお力添えによ
り実現しました。Katharine Muller 氏と David Muller 氏、
Yoshie Morimura 氏、Captain Satoshi Suzuki 氏、Peggy
Kline 氏と愛馬の Grady、Chiharu Lorenzoni 氏、Lance Tan
氏、Sergei Golubitsky 氏、Ginny Tapley Takemori 氏、Ta-
kuma Yamanaka 氏、Nobukazu Kawasaki 氏、Betsy Rogers

氏、Susan Griffin 氏、そして特に Gold's Gym の Jin さんと Sakai さんと彼らのチームの皆さんには、お時間をさいていただきまた親切にサポートしていただきました。心からお礼を申し上げたいと思います。

　とても幸運なことに、私には、女性としての強さと影響力を持ち、私を（ギリシャ神話に登場する）アマゾーンのように駆り立ててくれる母 Hélène Pancoast と義母 Ichiko Nagamura がいます。そして、まじめすぎる私の背中を押しつつそれに気づかせてくれる息子の Leo がいます。最後になりましたが、仕事場を提供してくれ、食べることを忘れてしまった私に食事を作ってくれる夫の Mitsuhiro がいます。実のところ、スポーツに使用される英語表現を軸にした本を執筆することを薦めてくれたのは夫なのです。まさかこの俳句集のことを思い描いていたということはないと思いますが、本書を気に入ってもらえたら大変光栄に思います。

Contributors

Barnabas I. Adeleke is a nature photography enthusiast. Among other awards, he won the Akita Chamber of Commerce and Industry President's Award in the 6th Japan-Russia Haiku Contest and Grand Prize in the 19th Haiku International Association Haiku Contest.

自然写真愛好家、第6回日露俳句コンテストにおける秋田商工会議所会頭賞や国際俳句交流協会第19回俳句大会で特選を受賞。

Elaine Andre has won many international haiku awards. Her design career includes the design and building of custom sailing yachts, hand-fabricated fine jewelry, textile mediums, and international *sumi-e* exhibitions—all of which distill line and image.

数々の国際俳句大会で賞を受賞。デザイナーとしてのキャリアは、オーダーメードのヨットの設計・建造、宝石の制作、布絵の創作、国際墨画展出展と豊富。

Terry Ann Carter is a poet and paper artist who lives in Victoria, British Columbia, Canada. She has published seven collections of poetry and five haiku chapbooks. A past president of Haiku Canada, she is the facilitator for Haiku Arbutus (Haiku Study Group of Victoria), and author of *Lighting the Global Lantern: A Teacher's Guide to Japanese Literary Forms* (Wintergreen Studios Press, 2011).

カナダ・ブリティッシュコロンビア州ヴィクトリア市在住の詩人・俳人・ペーパーアーティスト。詩集を7冊及び俳句集5冊を著作出版、Haiku Canada 前会長、ヴィクトリア市の俳句団体である Haiku Arbutus の創設者。著作『Lighting the Global Lantern: A Teacher's

Guide to Japanese Literary Forms』 (Wintergreen Studios Press, 2011)。

Kanchan Chatterjee is an award-winning, widely-published haijin from India. His haiku appeared regularly in NHK's program *Haiku Masters*, where he was chosen as "Haiku Master" several times.

受賞歴のあるインドの俳人。広く著作を出版。NHK放送の番組『Haiku Masters』において、俳句マスターに何度も選出される。

Marion Clarke's work has received awards, been published in International haiku journals, the *Mainichi*, *Asahi Shimbun*, and *Financial Times* newspapers and, by invitation, in two national anthologies of haiku from Ireland.

著作は受賞し、国際的な俳句誌や毎日新聞、朝日新聞、フィナンシャルタイムズ紙に掲載される。2冊のアイルランド俳句選集に収録される。

Terri Hale French currently serves as secretary for The Haiku Foundation. She is a past Southeast Regional Coordinator for The Haiku Society of America and former editor of *Prune Juice Journal* of *senryu* and *kyoka*. Terri was recently added to the editorial team of the online journal Haibun Today.

現在、The Haiku Foundation のセクレタリー。アメリカ俳句協会 南東地域の前コーディネーターであり、川柳や狂歌の雑誌『Prune Juice』の前編集者。近年オンラインジャーナル『Haibun Today』の編集チームに参加。

Abigail Friedman began composing haiku under the guidance of haiku master Kuroda Momoko. Since then, she has appeared in and authored many books, including *The Haiku Apprentice: Memoirs of Writing Poetry in Japan* (Stone Bridge Press, 2006). She is the founder of the Supernova haiku group of Washington, D.C., where she now resides.

俳人黒田杏子の指導の下で句作を始める。入門後、『The Haiku Apprentice: Memoirs of Writing Poetry in Japan』(Stone Bridge Press,

2006) など多くの著作を発表。現在ワシントン DC に在住、俳句グループ The Supernova を創設。

Goran Gatalica is a physicist who is a member of the Croatian Writers' Association. He has written poetry, haiku, and prose which are published in three books as well as many journals and anthologies.

クロアチア作家協会の会員であり物理学者。詩、俳句、散文など、3 冊の書籍のほか、多くの雑誌やアンソロジーに掲載される。

Nikolay Grankin was born in Tuapse, Russia. Now he lives in Krasnodar in the south of Russia. Nikolay has been writing haiku for about ten years, two of them in English. His haiku have appeared in some online and print journals in both Russian and English.

ロシアのトゥアプセ生まれ。現在はロシアの南部クラスノダール在住。俳句を始めて約10年、英語での句作も2年になる。俳句はオンラインあるいは紙媒体の雑誌でロシア語と英語で発表。

Lee Gurga is a past president of the Haiku Society of America and former editor of the journal *Modern Haiku* (USA). He is currently editor of Modern Haiku Press (USA).

Haiku Society of America 元会長、『Modern Haiku』(USA) 誌の前編集者。現在は Modern Haiku Press (USA) の編集者。

Kotaro Iizawa is widely considered one of Japan's most brilliant photography critics. Among his books are *Welcome to the Photography Museum* (Kodansha, 1996, winner of a Suntory Foundation Prize) and *Photographic Thinking* (Kawade Shobo, 2009). His latest publication, in 2018, is a collection of illustrations and haiku, titled *Reading the Moon*.

日本の傑出した写真評論家として広く知られている。数ある著書には『写真美術館へようこそ』(講談社 1996、サントリー財団賞受賞) や『写真的思考』(河出書房 2009) がある。2018年にはドローイングと俳句で編んだ『月読み』が出版された。

Masako Kakutani is a current member of the haiku group "Miraizu" and serves on the Board of Directors for the Society of Haiku Poets, and the Haiku International Association. She has three haiku books, *Honryu* (A Rushing Stream), *Geryu* (Headwaters), and *Chikasuimyaku* (Groundwater Vein), and two haiku review books, *Yamaguchi Seishi no 100 ku wo yomu* (Reading 100 haiku of Yamaguchi Seishi) and *Haiku no suimyaku wo motomete* (Search for Groundwater of Haiku), and has co-authored *Josei Haiku no Sekai* (World of Female Haiku Poets in Japan)."

俳誌『未来図』同人、俳人協会理事、国際俳句交流協会国際実行委員。句集『奔流』『源流』『地下水脈』、著作『山口誓子の100句を読む』『俳句の水脈を求めて』、共著『女性俳句の世界』。

kris (moon) kondo, who arrived in Japan by ship in June 1972, is an artist, poet, teacher, jewelry maker, and granmama who lives in a mountain village west of Tokyo.

1972年に船で日本に到着。アーティスト、詩人、教師、宝石制作者であり、東京西側の山村に居住するおばあちゃん的存在でもある。

Leonardo Lazarri lives in Baronissi, Italy, where he reads, studies, and writes. In 2018 he co-founded the website Yoisho to promote the haiku culture in his country. His works regularly appear in international magazines and win awards.

イタリア、バロニッシに在住。読書、研究、詩作を行う。2018年にイタリアで俳句を広めるために立ち上げられたウェブサイトYOISHOの共同創立者。国際的な雑誌に継続的に掲載、国際大会の常連受賞者。

Greg Longenecker is a widely published poet, two-time winner of the H. Gene Murtha Senryu Contest, and author of *Somewhere Inside Yesterday*.

詩集を広く出版、H. Gene Murtha川柳コンテストで2回受賞、『Somewhere Inside Yesterday』の著者。

Carole MacRury is the author of *In the Company of Crows: Haiku and Tanka Between the Tides* (Black Cat Press, 2008) and *The Tang of Nasturtiums*, an award-winning e-chapbook (Snapshot Press

2012). Her poems have won multiple awards and been published worldwide.

『In the Company of Crows: Haiku and Tanka Between the Tides』 (Black Cat Press 2008) 及び、e-chapbook 受賞の『The Tang of Nasturtiums』(Snapshot Press 2012) の著者。数々の受賞歴に輝く著作を世界各国で出版。

Marie Mariya is a haiku poet, literary critic, an executive committee member of the Haiku International Association, and a member of the Association of Haiku Poets. She served on the Selection Committee of *Haiku Masters*, the NHK World TV program, and has recently finished, with her sister, a back-translation of the entirety of Arthur Waley's *Tale of Genji*.

俳人、文芸評論家、俳人協会会員、国際俳句交流協会実行委員、NHKワールドTV『Haiku Masters』の選者。近著に『源氏物語 ウェイリー版』(左右社) 毬矢まりえ＋森山恵姉妹訳がある。

David McCullough has studied karate in Europe and Japan for more than twenty years. He is a long-term member of the Hailstone Haiku Circle in Kyoto.

日本並びに欧州で空手を20年以上学ぶ。ヘイルストーン俳句サークル京都の長年にわたる会員。

Marietta McGregor is an internationally-published Canberra poet. A retired botanist/journalist and photography enthusiast, her haiku, haibun, and photo-haiga have won awards in Australia, Japan, the U.S., Canada, Ireland, and the U.K.

世界的に著作が出版されているキャンベラ在住の詩人。植物学者・ジャーナリストを退職し写真愛好家である。彼女の俳句、俳文、写真俳句はオーストラリア、日本、米国、カナダ、アイルランド、英国で受賞歴がある。

David McMurray teaches at the International University of Kagoshima. He has curated 25,000 haiku during the past quarter century of editing the Asahi Haikuist Network column for the *Asahi Shimbun*.

鹿児島国際大学教授。過去四半世紀の間に朝日新聞Asahi Haikuest Networkのコラムで2万5千におよぶ俳句を編纂。

Yoshie Miyaji is a native of Tokyo who began taking private calligraphy lessons from age six. She holds the title of Shodo Shihan (Master Calligrapher) at Nihon Shodo Kenkyukai and also at Rinchikai.

東京生まれ、6歳より書道を始める。日本書道研究会及び臨池会の書道師範。

Emiko Miyashita was born in Fukushima, Japan in 1954, and currently lives in a traditional home in Tokyo. She studied with Dr. Akito Arima and Dr. Akira Omine, and is an active member of HIA, Haiku Poets' Association, and Haiku Canada, and is widely published.

1954年福島生まれ、現在は東京の伝統的住宅に居住。物理学博士で俳人有馬朗人及び哲学者で俳人大峯顕に俳句を学ぶ。国際俳句交流協会評議員、俳人協会幹事、カナダ俳句協会会員、著書多数。

Megumi Moriyama is a poet, English haiku poet, and translator. She is the author of four full-length books of poetry, was selected as a New Poet by a major poetry periodical in Japan, and has appeared in numerous journals and anthologies. She served on the Selection Committee of *Haiku Masters*, the NHK World TV program, and has recently finished, with her sister, a back-translation of Arthur Waley's the *Tale of Genji*.

詩人、英語俳句の俳人、翻訳家。自身の詩集を数多く著作、日本の主要な詩・短歌・俳句雑誌の新人賞受賞。多くの雑誌、選集に掲載、NHKワールドTV『Haiku Masters』の選者。近著に『源氏物語 ウェイリー版』（左右社）毬矢まりえ＋森山恵姉妹訳がある。

Michio Nakahara is a haiku poet and artist. He is the winner of both the Association of Haiku Poet's rookie award for *Touji* (Prodigal Son), and the Association of Haiku Poets award for *Rochou* (Top of the Head). He is the leader of the Ginka Haiku group, and a member of the Japan Writer's Association. He has published thirteen collections of his haiku.

俳人、第1句集『蕩児』により第13回俳人協会新人賞を受賞、第2句集『顳顬』により第33回俳人協会賞を受賞。「銀化」俳句会主宰、日本文藝家協会会員、これまで13の俳句集を出版。

Kazuko Nishimura was born in Yokohama, and graduated from Keio University. She heads the Chiin Haiku Group, and serves as a director for the Association of Haiku Poets and the Haiku International Association. Her books include a collection of haiku titled *One Chair*, and scholarly volumes such as *Reading the Genji Monogatari through Kigo*.

横浜生まれ。慶應義塾大学文学部卒。知音俳句会代表。俳人協会理事。国際俳句交流協会理事。句集『椅子ひとつ』著作『季語で読む源氏物語』ほか。

Kazuo Oda is a lifelong avid tennis player, and acquaintance of the Emperor Emeritus and Empress Emerita. He worked at Mitsubishi Corporation, and navigated the complicated days of the oil crisis. Today, he beats players many years his junior on the tennis courts.

現役テニスプレーヤー、天皇皇后両陛下と長年にわたりご交流がある。三菱商事で石油エネルギー分野を担当しオイルショックの危機を乗り切る。近年はテニスの後進の指導を続けている。

Junko Ochi is a former diplomat who was assigned mainly to cultural exchanges in Chicago, London, Oslo, Budapest, Helsinki, and Portland in the U.S. and European countries. She is a haiku poet member of the group Koshi, led by Kai Hasegawa and Hiroshi Otani.

シカゴ、ロンドン、オスロ、ブダペスト、ヘルシンキ、ポートランドなど欧米諸国で主に文化交流の分野において外交官として勤務。長谷川櫂や大谷弘至が主宰する「古志」の会員。

Natalia Rudychev has served as a judge for the Robert Spiess Haiku Contest and Resobox International Haiku Contest. Her book *Simple Gifts* (Red Moon Press, 2018) was shortlisted for the Touchstone Distinguished Book Award.

ロバート・スパイス俳句大会及びリソボックス国際俳句大会の審査員を務める。著書『Simple Gifts』(Red Moon Press 2018) は Touchstone Distinguished Book Award の候補リストに上がった。

Robin Anna Smith is an award-winning writer who has two haiku collections: *Systems Askew* (2019) and *Forsythia* (2019). Robin is the Chief Editor at *Human/Kind Journal* and Human/Kind Press.

数々の受賞歴に輝く作家。2冊の俳句集 Systems Askew (2019) と Forsythia (2019) を発行。Human/Kind Journal 及び Human/Kind Press の編集者。

Alan Summers is a *Japan Times* award-winning/Pushcart Prize-nominated writer, President of the United Haiku and Tanka Society, and has been filmed by NHK Television of Japan for *Europe meets Japan—Alan's Haiku Journey*.

ジャパンタイムズ社賞受賞、プッシュカート賞ノミネート作家。The United Haiku and Tanka Society 会長。『ヨーロッパ　日本と出会う──アランの俳句紀行』がNHKテレビで放送される。

Nanae Tamura is a haiku essayist and translator of Shiki Masaoka's work into English. She presented on Shiki's life at Boston University in 2017. She is also the co-author with Cor van den Heuvel of *Baseball Haiku* (W. W. Norton, 2007).

俳句エッセイスト、正岡子規作品の翻訳者。2017年ボストン大学で子規の生涯について講演。『Baseball Haiku』(W. W. Norton 2007) Cor van den Heuvel との共著者。

Akira Usami is the owner of the Kajikaen Museum, formerly a Japanese traditional inn operated for 100 years, in the Mitake Valley of Ome, Tokyo. He has contributed to the literary haiku magazines *Ten*, *Koma*, and *Haruno* and has traveled the roads and areas made famous by the writings of Matsuo Basho in the *Oku no Hosomichi*.

東京青梅市御嶽にある美術館「河鹿園」を経営。「河鹿園」は美術館になる以前は100年以上旅館として営業していた。俳誌に数々の俳句を寄稿、松尾芭蕉『奥の細道』の足跡を追体験した。

About the Author

Kit Pancoast Nagamura was born in Coconut Grove, Florida, took her
B. A. with honors at Brown University, and first visited Japan on a
Samuel T. Arnold fellowship, offered through the generosity of IBM's
Thomas J. Watson, Jr. She returned to the U.S. to take a Master's
at University of Michigan, where she won a Major Hopwood Award
for fiction, then received a Ph.D. with honors from the University of
Wisconsin-Madison. Back in Tokyo, she worked as both editor and
photographer, and began her long-running column for the *Japan Times*,
"The Backstreet Stories."

Nagamura has co-hosted NHK World's international TV show
Haiku Masters for three years, and is a member of the Haiku Interna-
tional Association, and the Ginza Poetry Society. She has won awards
of excellence from the Ito-en Oi Ocha Haiku Contest, the Yuki Teikei
Haiku Society, and the Setouchi Matsuyama Haiku Contest, among
others. She gives lectures and seminars on haiku across Japan and in
the U.S., serves as a judge for international haiku contests, and cur-
rently lives in Japan with her husband and son.

フロリダ州ココナッツグローブ生まれ。優秀な成績でブラウン大学卒業、
IBM's Thomas J. Watson, Jr. による Samuel T. Arnold フェローシップに
より最初の日本訪問の後米国へ帰国、ミシガン大学でフィクション分野
でホップウッド賞を受賞、同修士号取得、更にウィスコンシン大学マデ
ィソン校で優秀な成績で博士号取得。その後東京に戻り編集者・写真家
として活躍、『The Japan Times』の長期にわたる連載記事「The Back-
street Stories」の執筆を開始。

NHK ワールド TV の番組『Haiku Masters』で 3 年間共同司会者を担当、
国際俳句交流協会及び銀座英語句会の会員、伊藤園お〜いお茶新俳句大
賞、有季定型俳句協会、瀬戸内・松山国際俳句写真コンテストなど数々
の大会で優秀賞を受賞、日本及び米国で幅広く俳句関連の講演、セミナ
ーを実施、国際的な俳句コンテストの審査員を務める。現在夫と息子と
共に東京に在住。